What It Takes to Be

Number One

Vince Lombardi
& VINCE LOMBARDI JR.

THOMAS NELSON
Since 1798

NASHVILLE DALLAS MEXICO CITY RIO DE JANEIRO

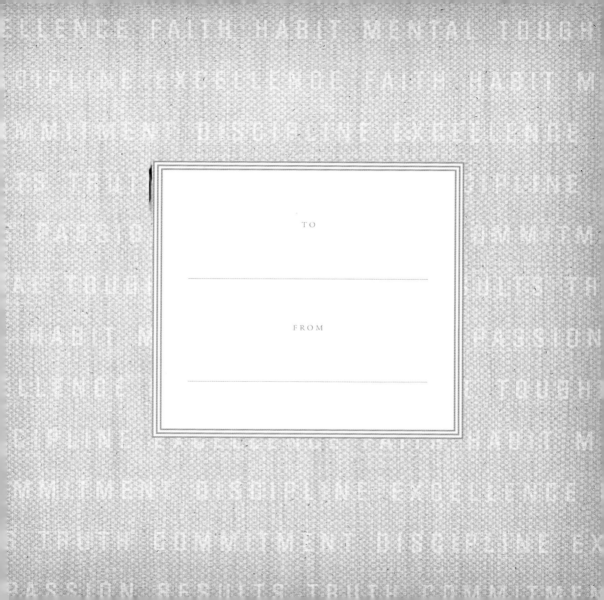

TO

_____

FROM

_____

My thanks to Vernon J. Biever,
whose photos are featured in this book.

What It Takes to Be Number One
© 2012 by Simple Truths

Published in Nashville, Tennessee, by Thomas Nelson. Thomas Nelson®
is a registered trademark of Thomas Nelson, Inc.

Originally published by Simple Truths LLC
1952 McDowell Road, Suite 300
Naperville, IL 60563
Toll Free: 800.900.3427
www.simpletruths.com

This edition published under license from Simple Truths exclusively for Thomas Nelson Inc.

Thomas Nelson, Inc., titles may be purchased in bulk for educational, business, fund-raising,
or sales promotional use. For information, please e-mail SpecialMarkets@ThomasNelson.com.

Unless otherwise noted, Scripture quotations are taken from: New Century Version®.
© 2005 by Thomas Nelson, Inc. Used by permission. All rights reserved.

ISBN: 978-1-4003-1997-8

Printed in Singapore

12 13 14 15 16 TWP 6 5 4 3 2 1

Contents

FOREWORD

I started Successories in 1988. The concept was simple: combine images with words to bring ideas to life. The excerpt from Vince Lombardi's famous speech "What It Takes to Be Number One" was our very first product, and more than twenty years later, it's still going strong. Lombardi was one of my heroes. There is something magical in those four hundred or so words that transcends football. The words, for me, capture the fundamentals of success—in any business or any life.

That's why I'm so excited about sharing this book with the rest of the world—a powerful combination of the words of Lombardi's famous speech with nine inspiring chapters from his son, Vince Jr.

I'm truly honored to be a part of bringing this timeless message to life.

Best wishes,

Mac Anderson

Founder, Simple Truths and Successories

Winning is not a sometime thing; it's an all-the-time thing.

You don't win once in a while;

you don't do things right once in a while;

you do them right all the time.

Winning is a habit.

Unfortunately, so is losing.

THERE IS NO ROOM
FOR SECOND PLACE.

There is only one place in my game,

and that's first place.

I have finished second twice in my time at Green Bay,

and I don't ever want to finish second again.

There is a second place bowl game,

but it is a game for losers.

It is and always has been an American zeal

to be first in anything we do, and to win,

and to win, and to win.

EVERY TIME A FOOTBALL PLAYER
GOES TO PLY HIS TRADE,
HE'S GOT TO PLAY
FROM THE GROUND UP—
from the soles of his feet right up to his head.
Every inch of him has to play.
Some guys play with their heads.
That's okay.

YOU'VE GOT TO BE SMART TO BE NUMBER ONE IN ANY BUSINESS.

But more importantly, you've got to play

with your heart, with every fiber of your body.

If you're lucky enough to find a guy

with a lot of head and a lot of heart,

he's never going to come off the field second.

RUNNING A FOOTBALL TEAM
IS NO DIFFERENT THAN
RUNNING ANY OTHER
KIND OF ORGANIZATION—

an army, a political party or a business.

The principles are the same.

The object is to win—to beat the other guy.

Maybe that sounds hard or cruel.

I don't think it is.

IT IS A REALITY OF LIFE
THAT MEN ARE COMPETITIVE
AND THE MOST COMPETITIVE

games draw the most competitive men.

That's why they are there—to compete.

The object is to win fairly, squarely, by the rules,

but to win.

AND IN TRUTH,

I've never known a man worth his salt

> *who in the long run, deep down in his heart,*

> *didn't appreciate the grind, the discipline.*

There is something in good men

> *that really yearns for discipline*

> *and the harsh reality of head-to-head combat.*

I DON'T SAY THESE THINGS

because I believe in the "brute" nature of man

    or that men must be brutalized to be combative.

I believe in God, and I believe in human decency.

But I firmly believe that any man's finest hour—

    his greatest fulfillment to all he holds dear—

      is that moment when he has worked

      his heart out in a good cause and lies exhausted

on the field of battle—victorious.

Vince Lombardi

(Entire Speech)

Winning is not a sometime thing; it's an all-the-time thing. You don't win once in a while; you don't do things right once in a while; you do them right all the time. Winning is a habit. Unfortunately, so is losing.

There is no room for second place. There is only one place in my game, and that's first place. I have finished second twice in my time at Green Bay, and I don't ever want to finish second again. There is a second place bowl game, but it is a game for losers. It is and always has been an American zeal to be first in anything we do, and to win, and to win, and to win.

Every time a football player goes to ply his trade, he's got to play from the ground up—from the soles of his feet right up to his head. Every inch of him has to play. Some guys play with their heads. That's okay. You've got to be smart to be number one in any business. But more importantly, you've got to play with your heart, with every fiber of your body. If you're lucky enough to find a guy with a lot of head and a lot of heart, he's never going to come off the field second.

Running a football team is no different than running any other kind of organization—an army, a political party or a business. The principles are the same. The object is to win—to beat the other guy. Maybe that sounds hard or cruel. I don't think it is.

It is a reality of life that men are competitive and the most competitive games draw the most competitive men. That's why they are there—to compete. The object is to win fairly, squarely, by the rules, but to win.

And in truth, I've never known a man worth his salt who in the long run, deep down in his heart, didn't appreciate the grind, the discipline. There is something in good men that really yearns for discipline and the harsh reality of head-to-head combat.

I don't say these things because I believe in the "brute" nature of man or that men must be brutalized to be combative. I believe in God, and I believe in human decency. But I firmly believe that any man's finest hour—his greatest fulfillment to all he holds dear—is that moment when he has worked his heart out in a good cause and lies exhausted on the field of battle—victorious.

Vince Lombardi

Whenever I speak, almost without exception, someone from the audience will come up after I'm done to tell me they have a copy of "What It Takes to Be Number One" in their office or den. One might wonder why. The speech is probably forty years old, and my father has been dead for over thirty-five years. What's at play here?

Well, some things are timeless, some things are enduring, and some things never change—things like the human qualities of commitment, excellence, discipline, and truth. My father had the fortunate ability to articulate his ideas about these enduring qualities in a "grab you where you live" kind of way. In addition, he compiled a winning record in a tough, competitive environment that would lead you to believe he knew what he was talking about.

I'm honored to be part of this book and to share the nine key principles that shaped my father's philosophy of coaching—and of life. I hope that in some small way it will help you reach your goals.

Vince Lombardi

VINCE LOMBARDI JR.

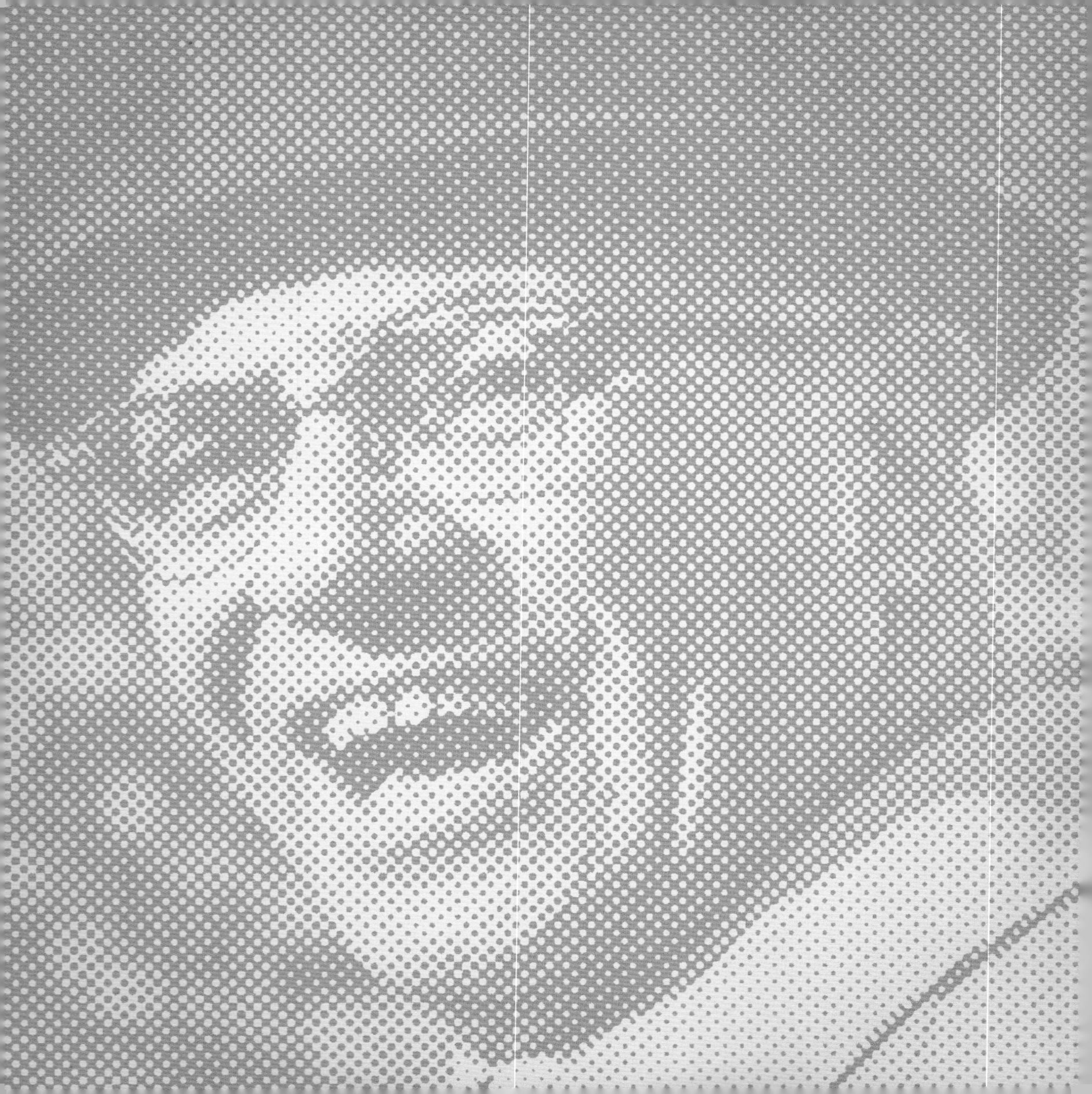

COMMITMENT

"Winning is not
a sometime thing;
it's an all-the-time thing.
You don't do things right
once in a while;
you do them right all the time."

It takes commitment for winning to be an all-the-time thing. It takes commitment to do things right all the time. Total commitment means 100 percent effort 100 percent of the time—no loafing, no idling, no standing around, no goofing off, no calling in sick.

When we make a commitment, in essence we're making a decision to do something. The Latin root for *decision* is "to cut away from," as an incision during surgery. So when we commit to something, what we're really doing is "cutting away" all other options, all other possibilities. When we commit to something, we cut away all the excuses, all the rationalizations.

Coach Lombardi confessed that it was hard to define commitment. He simply said, "It was all there was. There was nothing left." He just knew it when he saw it. Upon arriving in Green Bay, he felt that perhaps half the Packers players gave 100 percent most of the time. To win championships, he told them, it would take *all* of them giving 100 percent *all* the time.

Commitment—singleness of purpose—was the principal ingredient of the success of the Green Bay Packers, and no one was more committed to winning than Vince Lombardi. One of his Redskin players, Gerry Allen, said, "Everything about him is pushing toward a goal. He never stops, and he's going to have it. He's going to get it. I don't know who is going to be around to share it with him, but he's going to get it because he never lets up."

"THE QUALITY OF A MAN'S LIFE
IS IN DIRECT PROPORTION TO THEIR
COMMITMENT TO EXCELLENCE,
REGARDLESS OF THEIR
CHOSEN FIELD OF ENDEAVOR."

"Once a man has made a commitment to a way of life,

he puts the greatest strength

in the world behind him.

It's something we call heart power.

Once a man has made this commitment,

nothing will stop him, short of success."

Leaders make commitment a clear priority, leaving no room for misunderstanding. When my father arrived in Green Bay, he found very few Pro Bowl–caliber players. There was one such player, a wide receiver with considerable talent. But when Coach Lombardi spoke with the player, he got strong signals that the player's commitment was limited and would not be affected by anything the coach said or did. Before that player ever stepped on the field, he was traded to another team. The message to the other Packers players was clear: if you are going to play for Vince Lombardi, you are going to do it at a high level of commitment.

Sometimes Coach Lombardi's level of commitment was breathtaking. Once, as the Packers were preparing for a championship game to be played the day after Christmas, an assistant coach asked my father for a few hours off to do some shopping. He growled, "Do you want to be Santa Claus or a football coach? You can't be both."

When you commit to being an assistant coach at the professional level, you make a decision and you "cut away" all other options and possibilities. Banning Santa Claus may be an extreme example, but this incident is consistent with Coach Lombardi's sense of commitment.

"It's not whether you get knocked down; it's whether you get up."

Commitment

"I would say that the quality of each man's life is the full measure of that man's commitment to excellence and victory—whether it be football, whether it be business, whether it be politics or government or what have you." VL

DISCIPLINE

"I've never known a man

worth his salt who in the long run,

deep down in his heart,

didn't appreciate the grind,

the discipline."

Discipline can mean different things to different people. To Lombardi, it meant hard work and sacrifice. Hard work isn't just the number of hours invested or the blisters and bruises incurred. Hard work is discipline, the kind of focused effort that develops self-control. Discipline, born of hard work, helps you make the difficult decisions. It helps you embrace the pain associated with change. It helps you stay on track in the face of stress, pressure, and fear.

Discipline is also sacrifice, giving up one thing for the sake of another. Achievement involves choices, and choices mean sacrifice. Despite what today's advertisements tell us, you can't have it all. If you decide to get to the office an hour earlier to get your paperwork done before the phone starts ringing, you

must either sacrifice an hour of sleep or go to bed or get up an hour earlier (even if that means skipping your favorite late-night TV program).

Study the great performers in any field— music, theater, sports—and you will find that they all possess an enormous degree of discipline, a sense of duty. They have learned self-control, and they exercise it.

All too often, our culture celebrates success without any sweat. Our media tend to focus on people who achieve their goals in a seemingly effortless way—the "overnight success." There are no overnight successes! "No one who shuns the blows and the dust of battle wins a crown," said St. Basil. All those people we celebrate for their "effortless" success have

"Once you have established the goals you want

and the price you're willing to pay,

you can ignore the minor hurts,

the opponent's pressure, and the temporary failures."

actually put a lot of hard work and sacrifice into preparing for their moment of victory. They may make it look easy; they may even talk in a way that makes their achievement sound inevitable. But if you look and listen carefully, you will see, just below the surface, hard work and sacrifice.

A consistent theme for Coach Lombardi was "paying the price." He felt that achievement required the habits of commitment, mental toughness, passion, hard work, and the willingness to make sacrifices.

It stings and it hurts when you fall short of your goal. The Packers didn't win every game; nobody does. Sometimes you just want to crawl into a corner and lick your wounds. You don't want to think about work this weekend, and you certainly don't want to go to that Monday morning meeting with your VP or your manager. But that's the price you pay (hard work and sacrifice) to get into the arena.

> "WINNING IS NOT EVERYTHING—
> BUT MAKING THE EFFORT TO WIN IS."

"A man can be as great as he wants to be. If you believe in yourself and have the courage, the determination, the dedication, the competitive drive, and if you are willing to sacrifice the little things in life and pay the price for the things that are worthwhile, it can be done." VL

Discipline

EXCELLENCE

"I firmly believe

that any man's finest hour—

his greatest fulfillment of all

that he holds dear—is that moment

when he has worked his heart out

in good cause and lies exhausted

on the field of battle—victorious."

I end most of my speeches with this quote. Coincidentally, so do most of my father's former players whenever they have an opportunity to speak. Independent of each other, we have concluded that this quote embodies a significant idea.

What was it in my father's background, his upbringing, that prompted such thoughts as those contained in "What It Takes to Be Number One"? He was the son of hardworking parents who instilled in him the habits of discipline and sacrifice. At fifteen, he enrolled at Cathedral Prep, a high school run by the Catholic diocese of Brooklyn for boys who hoped to enter the

priesthood. Ultimately, he left Cathedral, feeling the priesthood was not his calling, but the church remained a central part of his life.

My father then attended Fordham University on a football scholarship. Fordham was an intense academic environment run by the intellectually rigorous Jesuit order of priests. The priests pushed him hard to think about the world and his place in it. The Jesuits believed that humans could perfect themselves through hard work and dedication to excellence. In the late forties and early fifties, my father was an assistant coach at the United States Military Academy at West Point, where duty, honor, and country were the codes of conduct.

"The spirit, the will to win, and the will

to excel—these are the things that will endure

and these are the qualities

that are so much more important

than any of the events themselves."

VL

I believe it was these three influences—the church, the Jesuits, and West Point—that formed the filter, the life philosophy, through which passed everything Vince Lombardi thought, said, and did. And it was this filter that caused my father to believe it wasn't enough to be a football coach. He saw himself more as a teacher, a "molder" of young men. He made his name in pro football, but I believe my father would have preferred to coach at the college level, where there were more opportunities for teaching and molding.

Coach Lombardi was very demanding of his players, assistants, family members, and everyone else who came into his orbit. He expected the most they could give and the best they could give. One thing he demanded above

"THEY CALL IT COACHING,
BUT IT IS TEACHING.
YOU DO NOT JUST TELL THEM . . .
YOU SHOW THEM THE REASONS."

everything else was personal responsibility. Being responsible meant being answerable and accountable for your actions and meeting your obligations and duties without prodding from a superior. Around him, you wouldn't even consider dogging it or "mailing it in." That was simply unthinkable.

He held his players to a particularly high standard. They were all gifted athletes who had a responsibility to use their talents to the fullest. "I will try to make each of you the best football player you can possibly be," he told his players time and again. "I will try with every fiber in me, and I will try and try." This wasn't the passion of a coach trying to win football games. This was the philosophy of a teacher who felt that all of us have obligations we can't shirk or avoid.

Every so often, a player with talent who didn't have the habits would arrive at training camp. Everyone knew it was only a matter of time before Lombardi took the young player on as a personal challenge. My mother, Marie, described this molding process best:

"When Vin is challenged to try to make a great one out of a ball player, I can only feel sorry for the player. Vin is going to make a hole in his head and pour everything into it. When it starts, the player hasn't got any idea what he's in for, and he hasn't got a chance. He'll get hammered and hammered until he's what Vin wants him to be. You can't resist this thing. You can't fight it."

"Unless a man believes in himself
and makes a total commitment to his career
and puts everything he has into it—
his mind, his body, and his heart—
what is life worth to him?
If I were a salesman, I would make
this commitment to my company,
to the product, and most of all, to myself."

"After all the cheers have died down and the stadium is empty, after the headlines have been written, and after you are back in the quiet of your room and the championship ring has been placed on the dresser and all the pomp and fanfare has faded, the enduring things that are left are: the dedication to excellence, the dedication to victory, and the dedication to doing with our lives the very best we can to make the world a better place in which to live." **VL**

MENTAL TOUGHNESS

"If you're lucky enough

to find a guy with a lot of head

and a lot of heart, he's never

going to come off the field second."

Mental toughness—head and heart—was one of Coach Lombardi's favorite topics. He believed that mental toughness was the single most important quality a leader needed to develop in himself and in the people around him. Mental toughness is the ability to hold on to your goals in the face of the pressure and stress of your current situation. It's the ability to hold on—and to hold on to what you want in the face of what you've got. Mental toughness is the glue that holds a team together when the heat is on and helps them persevere just a little longer—which in many cases is just long enough to outlast the competition.

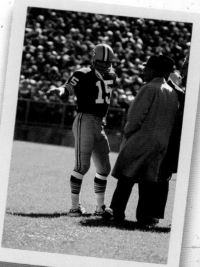

Coach Lombardi's brand of mental toughness dated back to his college days at Fordham University. He was an average player compared to some of his more talented teammates. He played mainly because of his determination. He once played an entire game with a cut inside his mouth that required thirty stitches to close after the game. He said, "I can't put my finger on just what I learned playing . . . but it was something, a certain toughness."

My father schooled his players in the mental approach to football, telling them, "Hurt is in the mind." He stressed that in order to win, they would have to disregard the small hurts, ignore the pain and pressure that would be applied by opponents and supporters alike.

In talking about mental toughness, Lombardi was emphasizing the necessity of staying the course when things start to go wrong. He was talking about using failure to come back stronger than before. We learn perseverance by persevering. "Sometimes it's good to have an obstacle to overcome, whether in football or anything," he once said. "When things go bad, we usually rise to the occasion."

> "TEAMS DO NOT GO PHYSICALLY FLAT;
> THEY GO MENTALLY STALE."

"Success is like anything worthwhile.

It has a price. You have to pay the price to win,

and you have to pay the price to get

to the point where success is possible.

Most important, you must pay the price to stay there."

"LEADERS ARE MADE; THEY ARE NOT BORN.
THEY ARE MADE BY HARD EFFORT, WHICH IS THE
PRICE ALL OF US MUST PAY TO ACHIEVE
ANY GOAL THAT IS WORTHWHILE."

Mental toughness is the ability to be your best at all times, regardless of the circumstances. It's easy to do well when there's no stress, but how many of us can be poised when the pressure is on? Mental toughness is constancy of purpose; it is total focus and emotional control. Mental toughness is not rigidity in the face of adversity; it is stability and poise in the face of challenge. Mental toughness is seeking out the pressure that can't be avoided and being energized by it. It's not just the ability to survive a mistake or failure; it's the ability to come back from failure stronger than ever.

Mental toughness isn't inherent. It's not something we're born with. Mental toughness is learned, just like every other quality it takes to be number one. We start small, achieving a minor goal. Then we set our sights higher, and we succeed again. We may not succeed every time, but if we work patiently toward our higher goals, savoring victories and shrugging off the small setbacks, we will prevail. And each time we raise the ante, we gain the skills and confidence that make the next success more likely.

Mental Toughness

"Mental toughness is many things and rather difficult to explain. Its qualities are sacrifice and self-denial. Also, most importantly, it is combined with a perfectly disciplined will that refuses to give in. It's a state of mind—you could call it 'character in action.'"

VL

Watch your thoughts; they become your beliefs.

Watch your beliefs; they become your words.

Watch your words; they become your actions.

Watch your actions; they become your habits.

Watch your habits; they become your character.

AUTHOR UNKNOWN

"Winning is a habit."

abits are those actions that get us through our day without a whole lot of conscious thought on our part. It's our habits, those actions that flow from our thoughts, beliefs, and words, that distinguish winners from everyone else. Dostoyevsky wrote, "It seems, in fact, as though the second half of a man's life is usually made up of the habits he has accumulated in the first half."

Where do our habits come from? The principal building blocks of habits are beliefs. A belief is your conviction that something is true and that you are in the "Belief Business." It is the quality of your beliefs—"This is the kind of person I am"—that determines your habits, which in turn, determine your character.

Beliefs are formed by self-talk. With this self-talk, you are constantly evaluating in a positive or negative manner what is

going on around you. Your focus is not on what is actually happening around you (the truth) but on what you *think* is happening, as you believe it to be. Over time, this self-talk accumulates into a positive or a negative opinion of yourself and your situation. This belief and opinion will subsequently be reflected in your words, actions, habits, and ultimately, character.

Of course, beliefs are only as good as the self-talk that created them (garbage in, garbage out). But good or bad, beliefs are the springboard for your words, actions, habits, and success.

"THE HARDER YOU WORK,

THE HARDER IT IS TO SURRENDER."

"The difference between a successful

person and others is not a lack of strength,

not a lack of knowledge,

but rather a lack of will."

Coach Lombardi was acutely aware of this self-talk connection—belief, action, habit—and he was constantly trying to influence his players' self-talk. Herb Adderley, Packers All-Pro cornerback, recalls Lombardi talking to him after a game against the Chicago Bears. "You just played the best game I've ever seen a cornerback play. This game was on national television. I'm sure the people who saw the game feel the same way. Keep this in mind—each time you go out on the field, say to yourself, 'I want these people, when they leave here, to say to themselves that they saw the best cornerback they have ever seen.'" Coach Lombardi was at work building the habit of winning.

"CONFIDENCE IS CONTAGIOUS

AND SO IS LACK

OF CONFIDENCE, AND A CUSTOMER

WILL RECOGNIZE BOTH."

Habit

"If you don't think you're a winner, you don't belong here."

VL

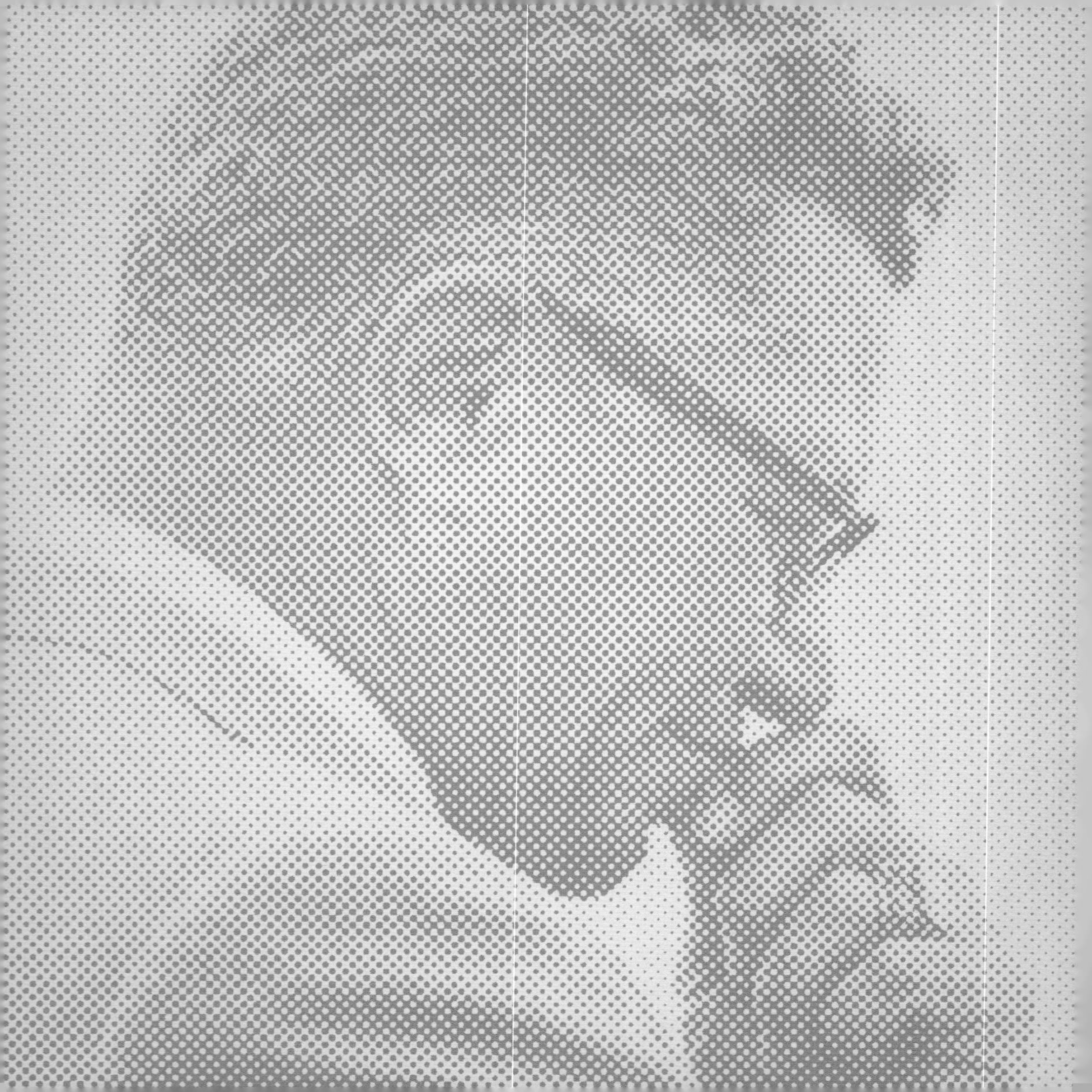

FAITH

"I believe in God."

The greatest gift my father gave me was the example of his faith. He attended Mass daily. His faith in God was his center, the source of his strength. He never wore it on his sleeve, and he never preached. A faith as strong as my father's doesn't need to be pushed on people; it was simply there, speaking for itself, making its point by example.

He refused the requests by journalists to allow them to photograph him praying in church. He suspected that such a picture would lend itself to abuse by a hostile editor, and he didn't want to cheapen his faith by appearing to trade on it.

Lombardi's faith was a personal tool for discovery, challenge, and renewal. He used his faith to conduct a dialogue with his Creator about the difficult paradoxes and contradictions of his life. He was famous; some people idolized him. Yet he didn't feel worthy of this kind of adulation. He set

extremely high standards for himself and those around him yet was well aware that all humans are fallible (particularly himself) and were unlikely to measure up to these high standards.

Bart Starr, his Green Bay quarter-back, once cracked, "If you heard Coach Lombardi at practice every afternoon, you'd know why he went to church every morning." It's a funny line, but it contains a lot of truth. My father wasn't comfortable being overly tough, pushing, pulling, demanding more from people than they believed they could give. But he knew that this behavior was largely responsible for his success. He went to daily Mass to talk to his God and to resolve these paradoxes and conflicts.

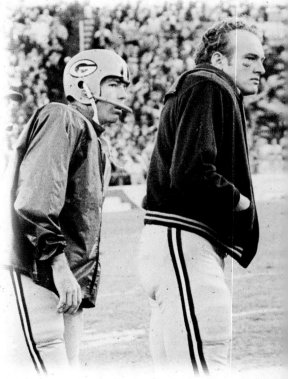

You can choose to ignore, stifle, or suppress your faith in a supreme being, but can you deny it? Each one of us must come to terms with faith—knowing what we believe and why we believe it.

Spirit is an essential part of our human nature. There is something in all of us that yearns for the universal, the unchanging, the transcendent. We are spiritual by nature. "We are not human beings having a spiritual experience," wrote Jesuit priest Pierre Teilhard de Chardin. "We are spiritual beings having a human experience." Many of our problems, stresses, and illnesses arise from ignoring the spiritual aspect of our humanity.

There is no situation or circumstance that is without a spiritual component. Every decision we make, every feeling,

every relationship we nurture has a spiritual dimension. The essence of life, the growth of wisdom and love, is spiritual. And sooner or later, most of us come to this realization, usually in our forties or fifties, after we have sought happiness in everything else—possessions, power, prestige—and found them wanting. At this point, we are finally willing to admit that true happiness lies in faith, in the spiritual journey.

My father's faith wasn't superficial or a faith of convenience. It was a far-reaching commitment that touched upon every aspect of his life. On the inside of all his championship rings are two etchings, one of the Sacred Heart of Jesus and the other of the blessed Mother holding the infant Jesus.

"I derived my strength from daily Mass and communion." VL

Faith

PASSION

"It is and has always been

an American zeal

to be first in everything we do,

and to win."

eal and passion are emotions that move you. Coach Lombardi was once described by late New York Giants owner Wel Mara as having "the zeal of a missionary." And although the Packers held a special place in his heart, my father's passion and enthusiasm extended beyond the team and into all corners of his life. He could get excited about dinner at a good restaurant, a sunset, Christmas with family, and especially a game of golf.

His passion overflowed. It was an enthusiasm that could be neither corralled nor fended off. "If you said, 'Good morning,' to him the right way," said a friend, "you could bring tears to his eyes." His emotional ups and downs as an assistant coach with the Giants earned him the nickname "Mr. Hi-Lo." A fellow coach once chided him for working up a lather over what seemed to be a minor football

matter. Lombardi said in response, "If you can't get emotional about what you believe in your heart, you're in the wrong business."

My father laughed and he cried. He communicated with every emotional tool at his disposal. "I've got all the emotions in excess," he said, "and a hair trigger controls them." Spontaneity was the saving grace for this hair-trigger personality. My father could yell at a player and five minutes later honestly not remember who he yelled at or why. People understood this and forgave him the excesses of his passion. Coach Lombardi never allowed his passion (and here we're talking about his temper) to become personal.

"IT IS ESSENTIAL TO UNDERSTAND THAT BATTLES
ARE PRIMARILY WON IN THE HEARTS OF MEN.
MEN RESPOND TO LEADERSHIP
IN A MOST REMARKABLE WAY,
AND ONCE YOU HAVE WON A MAN'S HEART,
HE WILL FOLLOW YOU ANYWHERE."

Passion and enthusiasm are the seeds of achievement. Enthusiasm is like an ocean tide—there's a certain inevitability about it. Zeal sweeps obstacles away. To motivate people, there must be a spark, some juice, desire, zeal, inspiration. It's tough to be a leader if you can't energize yourself and then your people. They need to be able to tap into your emotional energy—and you need to be able to tap into theirs.

"IF YOU AREN'T FIRED WITH ENTHUSIASM,
YOU'LL BE FIRED WITH ENTHUSIASM."

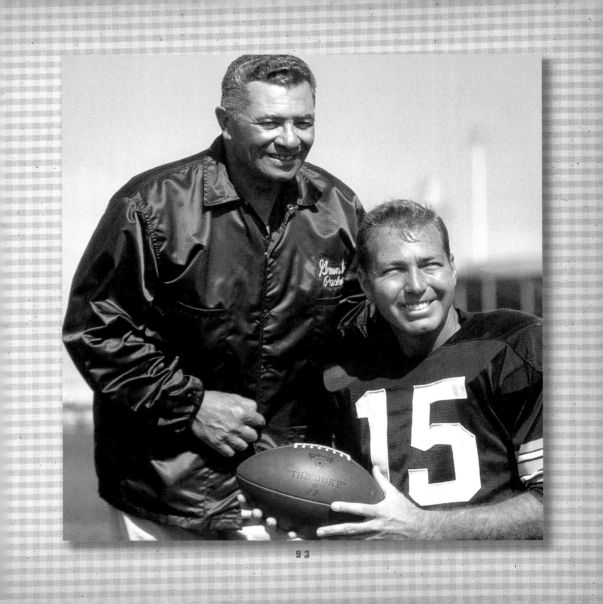

It's called *passion* today. In my father's day, it was called *emotion*. No matter what you choose to call it, I doubt you could find someone who was as passionate (and this is important) and as effective as my father. Having a plan is important, but along with a plan there must be hunger and a zeal to achieve the vision.

Few of us are inherently enthusiastic. Even Vince Lombardi had to give himself an occasional pep talk. For most of us, the passion to achieve, to be first, must be stoked. Every day, you must remember to lay on some kindling, strike a match, and fan the flames of passion and zeal.

"There's only one way to succeed in anything,

and that is to give it everything.

I do, and I demand that my players do."

"To be successful, a man must exert an effective influence upon his brothers and upon his associates, and the degree in which he accomplishes this depends on the personality of the man. The incandescence of which he is capable. The flame of fire that burns inside of him. The magnetism which draws the heart of other men to him." VL

Passion

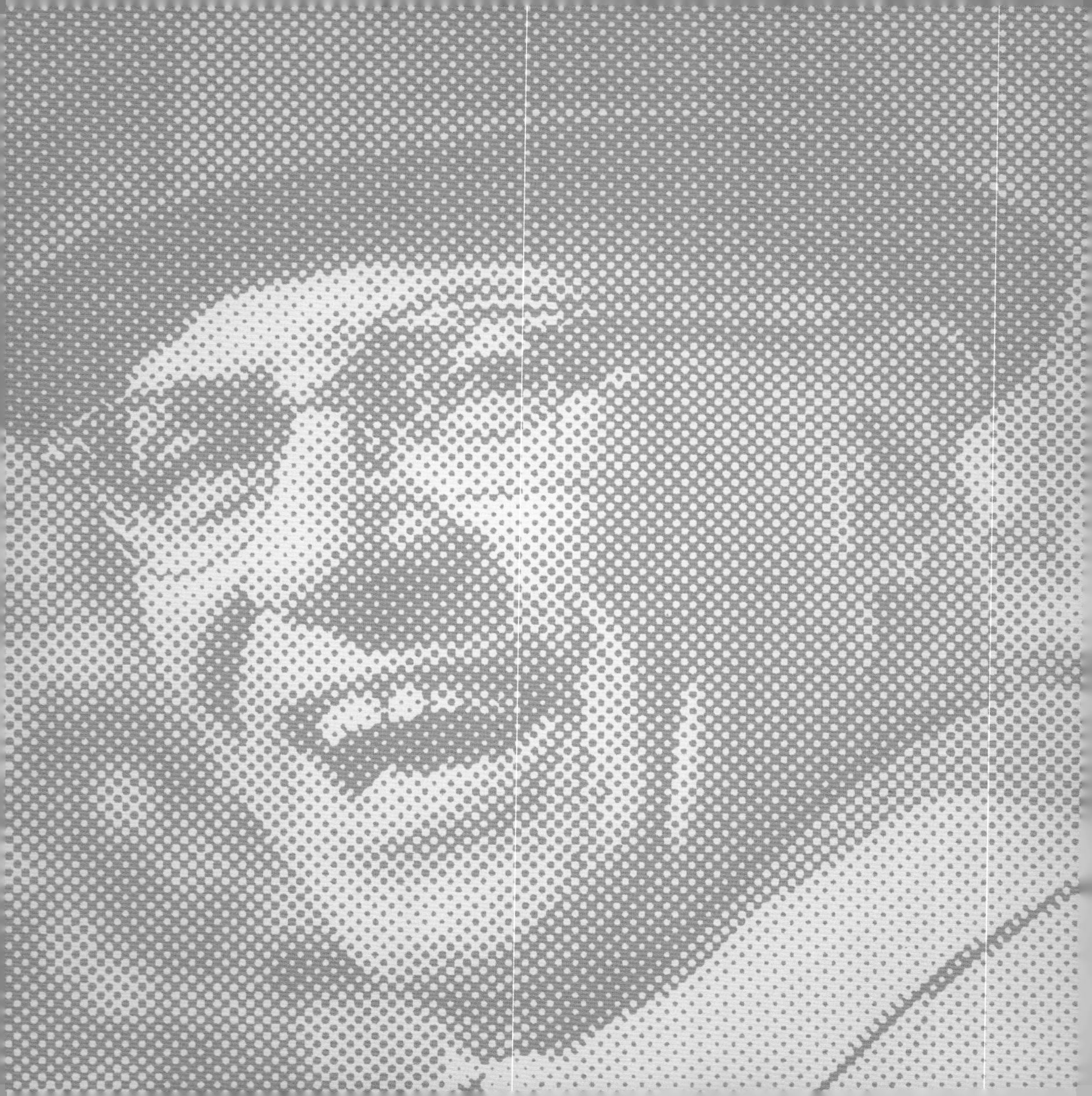

RESULTS

"Running a football team
is no different
than running any other kind
of organization."

Running a football team is no different than running a business. Results are the bottom line. It comes down to the consequences that are brought about by your leadership. The absence of positive results renders your leadership a failure. Bookstores are full of books regarding the debate about organizational structure: hierarchical or flat, centralized or decentralized, and everything in between. Yet it's not structure but results that make a leader. Leadership isn't a position; it's a process that produces the desired results. If you don't produce results, if you don't execute, you're not a leader.

Leaders get paid for results, not for being right. Results come from mistakes—being wrong—and leaders must possess Coach Lombardi's mental toughness to handle mistakes, take accountability for them, and quickly abandon efforts that fail to produce positive results.

If you are right all the time, you aren't taking enough risks. Results require a willingness to act, even if you are unsure of what lies ahead. And almost always, you will be unsure. Only through risk and action can you take your organization to the next level.

Results—specific and measurable—come from having a clear vision, defining what improvement and adaptation look like, and having a beginning and end in mind. Results come from knowing what you are achieving today and having a clear, specific strategy for closing the gap between today's reality and your vision for tomorrow.

Perhaps you don't want to be a Lombardi type of leader—challenging, demanding. Maybe you don't think you can be that kind of a leader. That's okay, as long as you produce results with whatever approach you feel comfortable with. But keep in mind that, ultimately, it's not whether people like you or approve of you as a leader; it's whether they produce for you.

"You never win a game

                    unless you beat the guy in front of you.

The score on the board doesn't mean a thing;

              that's for the fans. You've got to win the war

              with the man in front of you.

You've got to get your man."

In a training camp speech to the Packers players, my father told them, "I'm here because we win; you're here because we win. When we lose, we're gone." That's good career advice for *anyone* in a leadership role.

The ring the Green Bay Packers wear for defeating the Oakland Raiders in Super Bowl II has three diamonds across the face. They signify the three World Championships in a row the Packers had won, with Super Bowl II being the third. On one side of the ring are the words RUN TO WIN, from a verse Lombardi gave his players during the weeks leading up to Super Bowl II: "You know that in a race all the runners run, but only one gets the prize. So run to win!" (1 Corinthians 9:24).

Results

"Some of us will do our jobs well and some will not, but we will all be judged on one thing: the result." VL

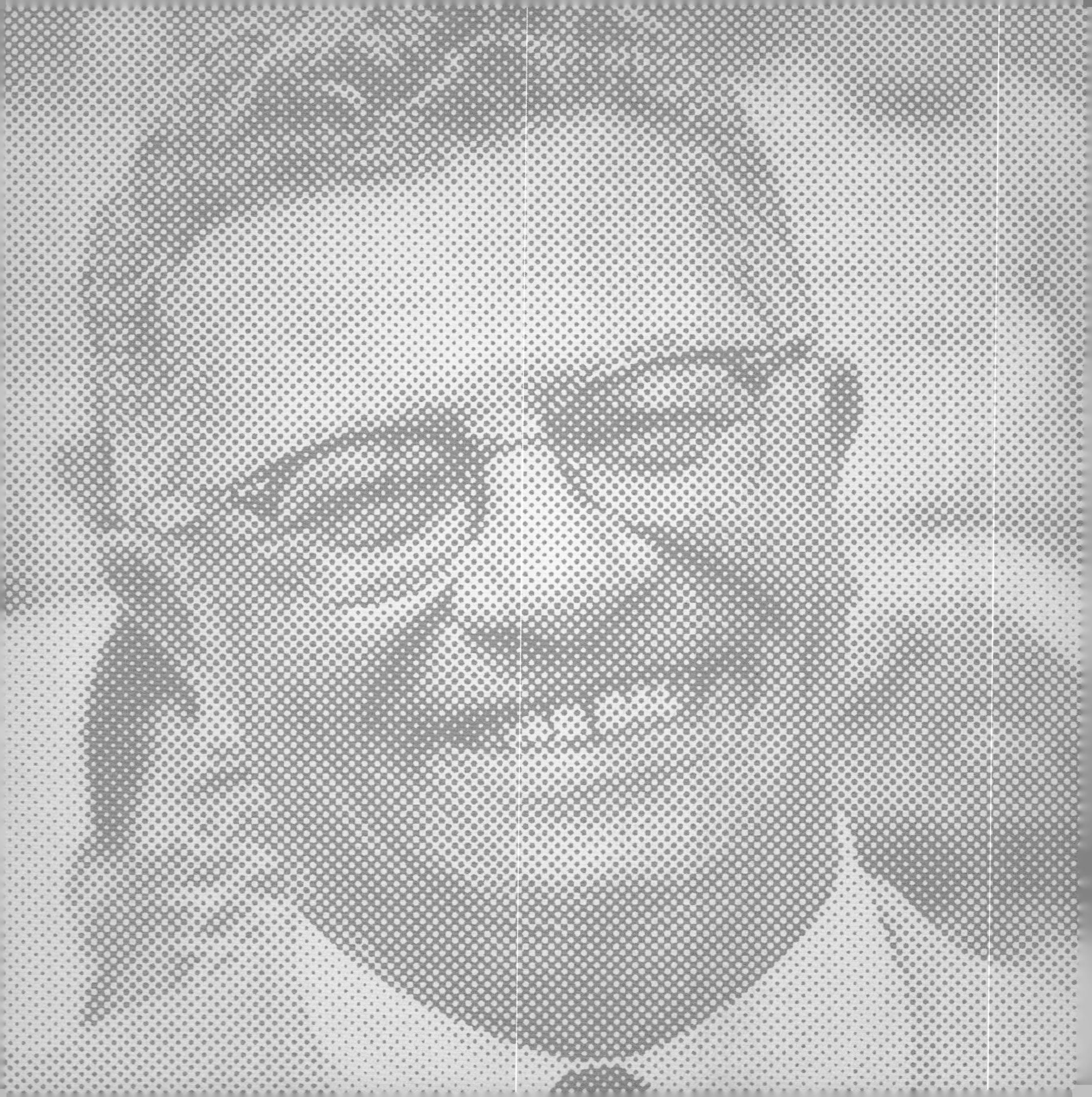

TRUTH

"The object is to win fairly,

squarely, by the rules,

but to win."

Fairly, squarely, by the rules—in other words, in accordance with the truth. Truth is best described by its opposites: lying, hypocrisy, and deception. Truth is an absolute necessity for a leader. Without truth guiding you as a leader, there's no trust. And if they don't trust you, you can't lead them.

So for a leader, what is true? For people like Vince Lombardi, objective moral principles constitute the truth. Customs and social mores may change, but fundamental truths transcend time and culture. And on a personal level, right and wrong are constant and unchanging. What is right today was right yesterday and will be right tomorrow.

Truth is determined through the filter of experience and personal reflection:

- The ends never justify the means.

- Values are not culturally defined.

- Values without morality mean nothing, because you stand for nothing.

- Not all values are equal.

• Life is cause and effect.
In other words, sooner or later,
you do sit down to a banquet of consequences.

• There are moral absolutes, which must take
precedence over social or economic expediency.

• Commitments are more important than self-interest.

• No self-interest is worth your reputation.

• It takes years to build a reputation
but only an instant to lose it.

• Truth is knowing that your character
is shaped by your everyday choices.

A person grounded in the truth does the right thing every time. When you are guided by the truth, you are the same person in private as you are in public. Looked at from the other end of the telescope, you know that what you do in private matters. Any talk of being able to "compartmentalize" your life so that your private actions have no bearing on your public life is fiction. You are no better than your principles.

What do you get with a person whose actions are grounded in the truth? One who knows the truth and follows it? Whose actions reflect the truth they believe in? Whose actions ring true? You get a person like Vince Lombardi—no hidden meanings, no dealing in the shadows, no backstabbing.

Organizationally, the truth is embodied in your values, how you conduct yourself in the public square. Values are the way people actually do things. Your agreed-upon values, based on the truth, determine the behaviors within your corporate culture. Once determined and decided upon, they are nonnegotiable. Truth and values get to the issue of professionalism, in a literal sense "professing" your values. In his first meeting with the Packers players, my father told them,

"You may not be a football player. You may not tackle. You may not be a guard. But you will be a professional."

Values come in two forms, espoused and practiced. The leader's challenge is to bring the two into alignment. Failure to do so leads to cynicism. "We say it, but we don't do it." This attitude eventually undercuts the leader's moral authority and credibility.

"We say it,

but we don't do it."

"Morally, the life of the organization must be of exemplary nature. This is one phase where the organization must not have criticism." **VL**

VINCENT LOMBARDI JR.

As the son of the great football coach Vincent T. Lombardi, Vince Lombardi Jr.'s early years were spent in an atmosphere full of success and achievement.

Armed with honesty, integrity, and authenticity—virtues he places above all others—Vince earned a law degree and maintained a private practice while serving in the Minnesota legislature.

He made the jump from law and politics to professional football in 1975, when he joined the fledgling Seattle Seahawks as an assistant to the general manager. He went on to become assistant executive director of the National Football League Management Council as a labor negotiator and later led two United States Football League teams as president and general manager. To each of these organizations Vince brought direction, enthusiasm, and the impetus to succeed.

Vince also brings that same passion to his speaking and writing. He has written five books and speaks sixty to seventy times a year on topics such as leadership, motivation, and team building. For more information, please visit vincelombardijr.com.

Vincent T. Lombardi

6/11/1913-9/3/1970